A CALL FOR REVOLUTION

THE DALAI LAMA and Sofia Stril-Rever

A CALL FOR REVOLUTION

A Vision for the Future

Written by Sofia Stril-Rever from private conversations with His Holiness

English translation by
Georgia de Chamberet & Natasha Lehrer

wm
WILLIAM MORROW
An Imprint of HarperCollins*Publishers*

 For information, address HarperCollins Publishers, 195 Broadway, New York, NY 10007.

HarperCollins books may be purchased for educational, business, or sales promotional use. For information, please e-mail the Special Markets Department at SPsales@harpercollins.com.

Originally published as *Faites la Révolution!* in France in 2017 by Editions Massot/Editions Rabelais.

FIRST WILLIAM MORROW HARDCOVER EDITION PUBLISHED 2018.

Library of Congress Cataloging-in-Publication Data has been applied for.

ISBN 978-0-06-286645-5

18 19 20 21 22 23 LSC 10 9 8 7 6 5 4 3 2 1

CONTENTS

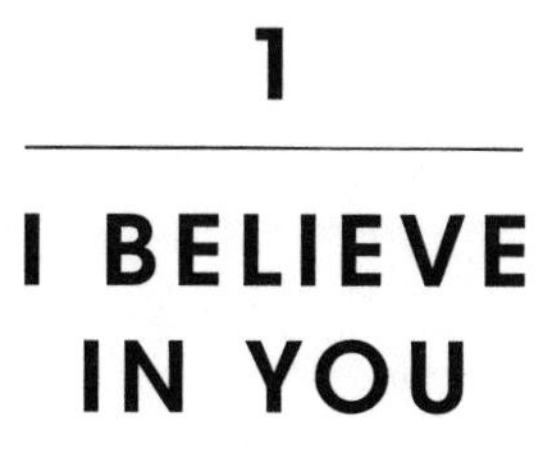

1

I BELIEVE IN YOU

My beloved brothers and sisters, my dear young friends.

You, the youth of today, are the generation born at the beginning of the third millennium. Our century is not yet twenty years old; it is still young, like you. The world is ageing at the same pace as you, and it will be what you make of it.

I am appealing to you having observed you keenly for some time. I have enormous faith in your generation. For several years I have organised meetings with you, both in India and on my travels to Europe, the United States, Canada, Australia and Japan. In the course of multiple exchanges with young people from all over the world I have grown increasingly convinced that your generation has the capability to transform this dawning century into an era of peace and dialogue.

You have the means of reconciling our fractured humanity both with itself and with the natural world.

Nonetheless, the potential for renewal exemplified by your generation is encircled by the shadows of the old world: a dark chaos of pain and tears. You must stand up to the wilful opposition to knowledge that is at large today, which is fraught with danger, where hatred, selfishness, violence, greed and fanaticism are threatening the very future of life on earth. I know that you have the persistence and strength to take on the future, and that you will succeed in drawing a line under the willed ignorance that you have inherited.

My young friends, you are my hope for humanity. I want to state it loudly and clearly so that you hear and respond to my message. I am confident in the future, for you have the capacity to lead humanity towards a renewed form of fraternity, justice and solidarity.

I am addressing you with the knowledge I have acquired through experience. I am eighty-two years old. At the age of sixteen,[1] on 17 November 1950, I lost my freedom, when I took my seat on the golden throne in Lhasa and accepted supreme authority, both secular and religious, over Tibet. At the age of twenty-five, in March 1959, I lost my country after it was forcibly annexed by the People's Republic of China. I was born in 1935, and have lived through many of the horrors of the twentieth century, the century that experienced the worst bloodshed in human history. However extraordinary human intelligence is, instead of serving, cherishing and protecting life, it has too often turned its ingenuity to destruction, even harnessing the force from which the sun draws its power. You were born into a world in which arsenals of atomic weapons have the capacity to destroy the planet dozens of times over.

Your grandparents and parents lived through two world wars and multiple conflicts that wrought bloody havoc on our world, and caused the deaths of 231 million people in the last century. Humanity was swept up in a tsunami of unprecedented violence, fed by fanatical nationalism, racism, anti-Semitism and ideological indoctrination. I was alive at the time of the Nazi holocaust in Europe, the nuclear firestorms in Japan, the Cold War, the wanton killing of civilians in Korea, Vietnam and Cambodia, and the Cultural Revolution and famine that caused the deaths of 70 million people in China and Tibet.

You and I have seen conflicts flare up in Afghanistan and the Middle East, devastating regions that were once the historic cradle of humanity. We have seen the images from the Mediterranean; its waves carrying the corpses of children, teenagers, women and men who drowned as they tried to reach Europe in the hope of a better life and of being able to help their families survive.

You and I are witnesses to the imminent breakdown of the earth's ecosystem, an alarming decrease in biodiversity, and the extinction of a plant or animal species every

I CALL ON
ALL YOUNG
PEOPLE
FROM ALL
OVER THE
WORLD

twenty minutes. We are silent witnesses to the massive deforestation of the Amazon – the destruction of the last great lung of our planet – as well as the acidification of our oceans, the bleaching of the Great Barrier Reef, and the melting of the ice packs in the Arctic and Antarctic. At the Third Pole, Tibet, the retreat of 46,000 Himalayan glaciers threatens to dry up the great rivers of Asia, sources of life for one-and-a-half billion inhabitants. Of all this you are only too aware. You were born into this world, and are growing up knowing about this spiral of destruction on a global scale, the result of war, terrorism and the ransacking of our natural resources.

THE EUROPEAN UNION, A MODEL FOR WORLD PEACE

Don't let yourselves be gripped by 'mean world syndrome'.[2] If you do, you run the risk of giving in to despair, of failing to notice that a global momentum for peace is gaining ground, thanks to an increasing emphasis on education in democracy and human rights. Never forget that genuine reconciliation is possible! Look at Germany and France. Since the sixteenth century these two countries have fought some twenty wars, climaxing in a paroxysm of barbarism in the two world wars of the last century. In 1914 and 1939, in Paris and Berlin, military convoys bore young soldiers to the front. They were your age, and had no idea of the atrocities that awaited them on the battlefield and in the mud of the trenches, or of the horrors of the death camps. A decimated generation of young men, grieving families, millions of orphans, countries in ruins, civilisation on its knees.

Yet it is precisely in these formerly warring nations that the desire for peace has won out against hawkish patriotism. The visionary leaders Konrad Adenauer and Robert Schuman laid the foundations for the European Union, buoyed by their consummate belief in fraternity and solidarity.

MY YOUNG
FRIENDS,
YOU ARE
MY HOPE
FOR
HUMANITY

Other political leaders have carried on their work, based on the principle of dialogue, in order to heal the wounds of so many people caught in the crossfire of conflicts all around the world.

The European model gives me genuine hope for your generation. Its dynamic of peace embodies the new reality in which this century is heading, a dynamic that even the rise of nationalism in certain member states will not be able to halt. As you know, there are already many organisations based on the European Union model being established in different regions around the world.[3] You too can play a part in helping these countries advance towards increased integration in order to minimise the risk of conflict. You too can play a part in promoting democratic values and basic freedoms throughout the world, helping different countries make inroads into ungovernable areas on every continent. I urge you to consider how you can be involved in increasing this 'spirit of union' worldwide.

Young Africans, you can help strengthen the African Union, which is bringing together all the countries on your vast continent. Young Americans and Canadians, you can build a North American Union. Young people of Latin America, a Latin American Union; and the youth of Asia, an Asian Union. On an international level, this will give the UN a far greater chance of bringing to life the beautiful slogan in the preamble of its founding charter: 'We, the peoples of the united nations'.

BERLIN, NOVEMBER 1989: YOUTH, PEACE AND DEMOCRACY

Allow me to share with you an unforgettable memory from November 1989, almost thirty years ago. You may not remember that at the time Germany was divided into two hostile states that were separated physically by a 100-kilometre-long, three-metre-high concrete wall. It was known as the Wall of Shame. Peppered with watchtowers, it divided individual families as well as an entire nation.

I happened to be in Berlin at the very moment when tens of thousands of young and enthusiastic demonstrators broke through the wall with their bare hands, knocking down frontier posts one by one, entirely peacefully. The whole world held its breath. Young people were changing the course of history. In both East and West Germany, this generation turned its back on ideological confrontation, affirming its desire for German reunification, a reconciliation made possible by a politics of transparency, set in motion in 1986 by my friend Mikhail Gorbachev, then leader of the Soviet Union. He refused to give the order to fire on the demonstrators and later declared that the fall of the Berlin Wall had avoided a Third World War.

I feel very emotional thinking back to the moment when I arrived, candle in hand, at the site where the wall had been breached.

The jubilant crowd lifted me up onto the rubble. It was an extraordinary moment, and I felt the breath of peace and freedom exhaling throughout the world. I was asked if I would like to make a statement. I simply said that just as the fall of the Berlin Wall had only yesterday seemed impossible but today had become a reality, so freedom would one day return to Tibet.

The symbolic impact of this momentous event was made even more significant by the fact that in March of the same year I had seen horrendous images of the bloody repression of peaceful demonstrations in Lhasa. Three months later, in June, tanks had crushed the student uprising in Beijing's Tiananmen Square. But in November, the fall of the Berlin Wall proved that it was possible for young people to proclaim non-violent victory against an oppressive dictatorship. When I reflect back on it today, that event stands as an epilogue to the tragedies of the twentieth century. By confirming the imminent demise of communism in Eastern Europe, it put an end to the legacy of the Second World War. The collapse of totalitarian regimes reinforced my belief that young people today are committed to universal values of democracy and solidarity. The consequences of the bloody 1917 Russian Revolution, which set in stone the USSR's future for the following seven decades, were effectively swept away thanks to this youthful pacifist insurrection, in the course of which not a single drop of blood was spilled.

TOPPLE THE REMAINING WALLS OF SHAME

Today, in the early years of the twenty-first century, I am launching an appeal to young people all over the world to break down the remaining Walls of Shame, not least those that have been erected in your minds. Walls of selfishness, walls of nationalist pride, of the cult of individualism, of pride and greed.

Everything that divides belongs to the past. All those forces of separation and exclusion will be powerless to resist the strength of the desire for peace embodied by your generation.

On a practical level, it can occasionally seem as though aggression is necessary: that a conflict will be resolved more quickly through the use of force. But when violence is used, the resolution that is achieved comes at the expense of people's human rights, safety and security. The problem will not truly have been resolved, but merely suppressed, and it will inevitably eventually resurface. History shows us that military victories and defeats are not lasting. This is true also in our own lives, in the context of family and friends. Without a rational argument, one allows oneself to become overwhelmed by anger and violence, though these are actually signs of weakness. Use your intelligence and make note of your mental reactions. When you are angry, you are animated by a blind energy that eclipses the astonishing human

YOU CAN
PLAY A
PART IN
PROMOTING
DEMOCRATIC
VALUES
AND BASIC
FREEDOMS

ability to distinguish between what is true and what is false. My friend, the American psychiatrist Aaron Beck, once explained to me that ninety per cent of the negativity that is attributed to the person or the object of our anger is comprised of our own negative mental projections. Pay close attention to your reactions and you will never again be overwhelmed by negative emotions. To understand is to free yourself and make peace with others. Seeking recourse in reason allows you to banish anger and its consequences, aggression and violence.

It is essential that you examine your deepest motivations and those of your opponent or adversary. Sometimes you will find it hard to choose between violence and non-violence. Don't forget that negative motivation will always result in a wounding or destructive act, even if in form and appearance it appears benign. Conversely, if your motivation is sincere and altruistic, it will always result in non-violent and positive acts.

Only an enlightened compassion can ever justify the use of force as a last resort.

Western people tend to take a different approach. According to them, non-violence and peaceful resistance are more appropriate to Eastern cultures. More inclined to action, they tend to seek immediate and tangible results in all situations. This attitude, which can be efficient in the short term, is often counterproductive in the long term, while non-violence, which demands patience and determination, is always constructive. The fall of the Berlin Wall and the liberation movements born in the countries of the former Soviet Union are highly instructive in this respect. It is also worth noting that in June 1989, Chinese students, born and educated under the yoke of the communist regime, spontaneously put into practice a strategy of peaceful resistance, so dear to Mahatma Gandhi. They remained peaceful in the face of the brutality of the regime's repression. Even though they had been indoctrinated, they chose the path of non-violence.

WAR, A COMPLETE ANACHRONISM

Non-violence is a pragmatic solution to contemporary conflicts. In spite of having experienced war and repression in my own country, where for over sixty years the People's Armed Police has enforced a reign of terror under orders from Beijing, stifling the freedom and dignity of the Tibetan people, I remain an ardent spokesman for world peace. Everything that I write is for the purpose of explaining how to create the conditions necessary for peace, both within each of us and all around us. If I did not believe in the possibility of peace, I would not be able to continue this conversation.

War today is a complete anachronism. Legally, we no longer even declare war, and in some countries all that is required to authorise military operations is a parliamentary vote. The old bellicose ideologies are outdated and every armed conflict provokes demonstrations for peace in major cities around the world. I rejoice when I see you, in your tens of thousands, rallying in solidarity for the causes of reconciliation and human rights. Witnessing huge numbers of young people demonstrating in support of humanitarian issues fills my heart with joy. Thanks to the rapid development of information technology, you are the first generation of truly global citizens. Learn to use social networks with discernment to speed up and spread awareness without letting internet and online gaming become a drug that you cannot do without! Be sure to transmit independently verified information in the service of truth and ethics. Be careful not to spread fake news. As digital natives, you were born world citizens, for digital culture has no borders. Is it not the case that in your minds, young people from all over the world are your friends, companions and

LEARN TO USE SOCIAL NETWORKS WITH DISCERNMENT

partners, rather than your competitors, rivals and enemies? It is undoubtedly true that war is part of human nature. But the genocides of the past century made your parents and grandparents mindful, and led them to cry, 'Never again!' It was they who showed that it is possible to resolve human conflicts through dialogue and non-violence.

You might well object to what I am saying by pointing out that even today, in the twenty-first century, we are still witnessing a tidal wave of conflicts that world powers persist in trying to resolve by force. The military machine remains a legal institution, and there are those who still consider war to be acceptable rather than a criminal enterprise. A form of brainwashing keeps people from recognising that war is by definition monstrous. It is the great paradox of our time: there is no more war, in the legal sense, yet violent crises and carnage are increasing. Young people have been the targets of violent terrorist attacks. Paris, November 2015, Parkland, Florida,

March 2018 . . . I was terribly disturbed by those events. They felt like murderous attacks on my heart. Young people slaughtering other young people! It was unbelievable, unbearable. These attackers were not born terrorists. They became terrorists, manipulated in the name of a fantasy, an archaic and brutal fanaticism that compelled them to believe that it is glorious to destroy, punish and terrorise.

Do not be discouraged. Your mission is to draw lessons from the errors of the past, all the while developing a dialogue of tolerance and non-violent communication with those around you. When you are confronted by violence, you must not give in to the kind of fear that blinds people with bitterness, anger and a thirst for vengeance. Take inspiration from the Norwegian prime minister who, in the wake of the July 2011 terrorist attacks in Oslo and on the island of Utøya, declared that his government would respond to terror with increased democracy, openness and tolerance. It is precisely by guarding against internecine hatred that you will become the architects of peace. The day is near when your generation will have consigned war to the ash heap of history. Perhaps when that day comes you will remember these words.

2

REBELS FOR PEACE

At eighty-two, I am ready to say my goodbyes. According to my age, I am a man of the twentieth century, but my yearning for peace, so deeply rooted in me, makes me feel that I belong more to the future of the world, and to the younger generation. In that sense, you and I are the same age, the age of renewal. The end of my life and the first part of yours are at a crossroads. The point where our paths join is like that brief moment when night and dawn meet in the sky. It is no longer night, but it is not yet daybreak. A new day is being born. It is as though one page is turning on the horizon to the next one. It is up to you, my young friends, to write the next chapter of our history. I hope it will be the most beautiful and joyful chapter in the entire memory of humankind.

I have been awaiting a peaceful future since the days when I lived in the country of my birth, Tibet. As an adolescent, all I knew of other countries was from the illustrated magazines that I read avidly in Lhasa. During my first journey to India, in 1956, travelling by yak and on horseback, I thought I might be lucky enough to catch a glimpse of the skyscrapers of New York from the top of one of the mountains of Tibet, the highest on earth. I hoped to be able to see it through the bronze telescope that I had inherited from my predecessor, with which I could see the craters of the moon from the terrace of the Potala Palace. Since then I have seen for myself modern civilisation and I have even played a small part in how attitudes have evolved, but I have remained steadfastly engaged with my early commitment to the cause of peace. From my perspective of having spent my life observing the world, I beg you to pay heed when I say that if your generation sinks into violence, you will see the death throes of humanity. The twenty-

BE CAREFUL
NOT TO
SPREAD
FAKE NEWS

first century will be the century of peace, or humanity will cease to be.

I call on all young people from all over the world to be the first generation on an earth that declares itself committed to peace and the good of all humankind. Build a global citizenry! Do not strive for utopia – make it a strategic objective, for it is the personal responsibility of each of you to ensure that the twenty-first century will not see a repeat of the suffering, devastation and bloodshed that characterised the past.

Youth of the world, you are the citizens of tomorrow's world. I am convinced that through your spirit you will be able to bring about global peace and fraternity, the greatest aspiration of the human heart.

BE THE SOLUTION-FINDING GENERATION

The problems that you face today were not created by you. My generation and that of your parents, those born in the twentieth century, are the problem generations. You must be the solution-finding generation! Your parents did not intend to damage the environment. We have only realised the extent of the catastrophe now that it is almost too late. Why? Because the degradation of the natural world has become visible only gradually, and for a long time was undetectable. In 2011, I invited international specialists to Dharamsala for a conference about ecology, ethics and interdependence.[4] One of the guests made the point that it is a shame that CO_2 is colourless and odourless. If it were blue or pink and had an odour we would be aware of it, and both politicians and the public would soon realise the danger of its increasing concentration in the atmosphere. I said, jokingly, that we ought to put all the world leaders into a locked room into which CO_2 is being piped, just long enough and in sufficient quantity that they begin to have trouble breathing and feel increasingly uncomfortable – obviously not in order to suffocate them, but simply to make them aware of the problem so that they would go away and take urgent measures to protect the planet. For the first time in human history, your right to life, and the right to life of your children, is no longer secure.

I want to congratulate a group of young Americans aged between nine and twenty for taking an initiative in the name of future generations. This group of teenagers is fighting for the fundamental constitutional right to live in an environment free of greenhouse gas emissions.[5] The judge agreed with their claims, using arguments based on scientific research: the concentration of CO_2 in the atmosphere means that there is no longer any guarantee that babies born in this millennium will reach adulthood in good health. This kind of lawsuit is not limited to the United States. An international movement for climate justice has arisen across the world, from North America to the Philippines, from

New Zealand to India to Norway, demanding that governments and big businesses take responsibility for their impact on the environment. You, today's young citizens, are pioneering climate justice, aware of the fact that you are directly concerned and it is your future that is at stake.

The fact that so many of you are engaged with these issues gives me confidence in my optimism for the future. The problems facing you, whether to do with climate change, violence in general and terrorism in particular, were not created by God, Buddha or extraterrestrials. They did not fall from the sky, or rise up from the ground. Humanity is entirely responsible for being at the root of the problems that have caused these crises. Which is good news. Because if we have created these problems, it is logical to believe that we have the means to resolve them. The crises facing us today are not inevitable. Ask yourselves: 'What if fraternity were to be our response to these crises?'

I HAVE ADOPTED THE MOTTO 'FREEDOM, EQUALITY, FRATERNITY'

I remember the first time I ever heard about the French Revolution. I was a child, living in the Potala Palace in Lhasa, and I overheard people talking about the Russian Revolution. I was fascinated by what I heard, and later I took to asking the occasional foreign visitor to the palace to tell me more about them; they became my secular teachers, so to speak. I also remember the first revolution that I followed in real time from Tibet. It was the Hungarian Revolution of 1956. Geographically I was far away from Budapest, but emotionally I felt extremely close to the young insurgents.

I have been inspired by the ideas of the French Revolution that were adopted as the motto of the French Republic: *Liberté, égalité, fraternité.* I adopted the same motto. As a Buddhist, the aim of my spiritual quest is to free myself of the fundamental ignorance that has led to the notion that there is a

IT IS UP TO YOU, MY YOUNG FRIENDS, TO WRITE THE NEXT CHAPTER OF OUR HISTORY division between people and the natural world, which is at the root of all our suffering. Equality is another Buddhist principle, the belief that all sensitive beings, both human and non-human, have the same potential for enlightenment. We call the practice of equality impartiality or equanimity. And the last part of the motto is fraternity, the importance of love and compassion for others, which is cultivated in Buddhism on a daily basis. India's constitution has appended a fourth element to the motto: *Justice*. This is shrewd, for without economic and social justice, fraternity is no more than a noble but empty ideal.

As soon as I was sworn in as the secular and religious leader of Tibet in Lhasa, in 1950, my first political act was in support of my brothers. I had seen in the prison near the Potala Palace many convicts sentenced to be tortured with the 'cangue'. This is a heavy wooden board that is attached around the neck of the convict, so heavy and rigid that it can snap the vertebrae in the neck. I ordered a general amnesty throughout Tibet and then began the reform of our feudal society by establishing an independent judiciary. I appointed a committee to redistribute land and abolish the hereditary debt system that enslaved the peasant community to the aristocracy. But the Chinese occupied and rapidly took control of Tibet, imposing their anti-democratic version of modernisation on my country. In 1959 I had to flee because my life was in danger. It was not until I was in exile in India that I was able to establish a functioning democracy for our institutions. On 2 September 1960, in Dharamsala, the first politicians in the history of Tibet were sworn in. Later, I wrote a Constitution proclaiming the separation of powers, the equality of all citizens before the law, free elections and guaranteed political pluralism. Based on the universal declaration of human rights of 1948, this text laid the foundations for a secular state and transposed our spiritual values into a solemn commitment to non-violence and peace.

I had to use all my powers of persuasion for the Tibetan people to accept these reforms, which limited the traditional extent of my powers. Their reverence and excessive veneration for my office were an impediment to this, and I realised it would be necessary to educate them about democracy. It was only in 2011 that I was finally able, voluntarily and with great pride, to devolve political power and secularise our democracy in exile. Thus the Tibetan people did not have to rise up in revolution, unlike the French revolutionaries, who beheaded their king and sacrificed their own lives for the sake of democracy.

THE REVOLUTIONS OF THE PAST HAVE NOT TRANSFORMED THE HUMAN SPIRIT

Because I am the Dalai Lama of Tibet, people are surprised to hear me expressing political opinions. But I am a disciple of the French Revolution. Although I do not know in detail the course of the French Revolution, I like to remind people that it was those revolutionaries who gave the world the *Declaration of the Rights of Man and of the Citizen* and its great principles that inspired the Universal Declaration of 1948. You may not be aware that in Tibet today it is forbidden to possess a copy of this text. It is considered to be a seriously subversive act, amounting to a crime against national security, and subject to imprisonment and torture. It is important that you understand the revolutionary significance of this text. My sense is that, historically, French intellectuals have always had a tendency to think in an all-encompassing way, a universal vision and openness to the wider world. The most brilliant of them have truly rebellious spirits, with an acute critical sense, which is of crucial importance in the twenty-first century, given how vital it is that we turn our backs on the ideologies of the old world that have done so much harm.

Just as I am a disciple of the French Revolution, I am also a disciple of Karl Marx. Marx considered France to be the apotheosis of the revolutionary nation, and he explained the mechanism of the 1789 insurrection with great lucidity. The old regime was no longer in tune with the economic reality of the times, which led to a confrontation between social classes as they each struggled to secure the power and the privileges of the aristocracy. The same reasoning was at the root of the Bolshevik Revolution in Tsarist Russia. That too was a social movement demanding an end to the abusive exploitation of the proletariat. These struggles for emancipation and social justice meant revolution was inevitable as long as political leaders stood in the way of change. In terms of redistribution of wealth as well as solidarity, I consider myself to be a

IF WE HAVE
CREATED
PROBLEMS,
WE HAVE
THE MEANS
TO RESOLVE
THEM

Marxist and I deeply regret that first Lenin and then Stalin chose to pervert Marx's ideas, with the result that the communist ideal swerved towards totalitarianism.

It is vital to study history in order to avoid repeating the errors of the past. If you look at all the revolutions that have taken place throughout history, you see that they came about in reaction to conflicts of interest caused by hatred, anger and frustration that grew until they became uncontrollable and eventually triggered the revolutionary process. The French Revolution, the Bolshevik Revolution and the Cultural Revolution all led to violent bloodbaths, wanton destruction and extreme terror. They may have brought about the fall of political leaders and regime change, but they failed to radically transform the human spirit.

The revolutions that took place in the last part of the twentieth century were different to those earlier revolutions because they were pacifist in nature. Young people were peaceful revolutionaries. They are the inspiration behind my call to you to confront the challenges of our era by rising up and embarking upon a revolution that has no precedent in human history.

3

BRING ON THE REVOLUTION OF COMPASSION

In June 2017, I was invited by the University of California in San Diego to deliver a speech at its graduate commencement ceremony. The parents of all the Chinese students had made the trip specially. 'I am calling on you to bring on a cultural revolution of compassion!' I declared, remarking that students are far more purposeful nowadays. Calling for a Cultural Revolution of Compassion in 2017 is not utopian. Hence my appeal: 'Young people of the twenty-first century, bring on the revolution of compassion!' These words are not intended to be a formulaic consolation, or a hollow slogan. They are not the naïve dream of an elderly Buddhist monk who is disconnected from reality. When I call on you to bring on the Revolution of Compassion, I am calling for the mother of all uprisings to begin. Many remarkable individuals have called for different kinds of revolution: economic, technological, energy, educational, spiritual, ethical, inner; a revolution of the conscience and of the heart . . . all are motivated by the urgent need to create a better world. But for me, the Revolution of Compassion is the heart, the bedrock, the original source of inspiration for all others.

NOW IS THE TIME FOR COMPASSION

Why now? Because compassion is vital. It is a mistake to think of it as a noble ideal, a beautiful sentiment. You have grown up in such materialistic, individualistic societies that showing compassion may seem to you to be a sign of weakness. If we do so, we forget that, more than anything, it is the energy that sustains life. Right now, as I make this appeal, life on earth is being devastated. Two-thirds of the world's vertebrate species have disappeared. Everywhere – in the fields,

I AM
RESOLUTELY
FEMINIST

the oceans, the sky and the forests – life on earth is experiencing serious depletion. This is the sixth mass extinction after that of the dinosaurs 66 million years ago. It is having a dramatic effect on ecosystems and on our societies. And it is a direct consequence of human actions, whose effects are intensified by technology. Now is the time for compassion: we need to rethink the way we live on earth in order to preserve life.

Today, we understand the biological nature of compassion thanks to research in developmental, social and affective neuroscience to test emotions, feelings and interpersonal skills. These disciplines demonstrate that compassion has a positive impact on neurogenesis (the formation of new neurons), from gestation onwards, throughout our entire life. Conversely, aggression limits the development of neural circuits, destroying cells in brain structures and blocking the operation of certain genes.

Compassion has an essential role when it comes to cerebral growth and plasticity. It determines the balanced evolution of children and teenagers, as well as the optimal deployment of their intellectual, emotional and relational capabilities. In adulthood, compassion is essential both for personal fulfilment and mental health. Studies have shown that our states of mind modify how our genes operate. If we infuse our minds with compassion, we block the genetic stress response and modify the brain's biochemistry: loving-kindness generates happiness.

Parents, educators, paediatricians and psychologists know this intuitively. Nonetheless it is vital to gather objective evidence that to love and protect, to cherish and care, are intrinsic to the human species, and the very condition of its survival. Aggressive, destructive, brutal, angry or cruel behaviours are not only antisocial, but unnatural.

I HAVE A DREAM: WOMEN WILL BECOME NATIONAL LEADERS

Our mother plays a crucial role in our childhood: this is true for all seven billion of us living on this planet. As you know, you would not have survived without your mother's love. Such is the law of nature. Fathers play an important role too, but at the beginning of life, the mother is irreplaceable. She is closest to the body, heart and spirit of her child. It is she who bore you and brought you into the world. Experiencing this primordial link is decisive. As the child grows up, it feeds on maternal tenderness as much as it feeds on milk. It is now recognised that in the early childhoods of most antisocial people, there was a lack of maternal love.

I was born into an impoverished family living in a small village in a backwater of eastern Tibet yet I have always felt wealthy; my mother lavished her boundless love on me. I never saw the slightest expression of anger cross

THE WORLD
IS YOUR
HOME,
HUMANITY
IS YOUR
FAMILY

her face, and she always spread goodness around her. I think of her as my first teacher. It was she who conveyed to me the priceless lesson of compassion.

I call on the next generation of young women to be the mothers of the Revolution of Compassion that this century so desperately needs. You have a special role to play in creating a better world. It is often thought that women are more empathic and sensitive, and more receptive to the feelings of others.[6] These are qualities that are embodied by mothers. In this sense, women are models of humanity. Study history, and you will see that throughout every era, across all five continents, it is men who have been responsible for carnage and destruction. They have been celebrated as heroes, when they should have been condemned as criminals!

The law of the strongest was already in force in prehistoric times. The muscular power of men in relation to women endowed them with physical superiority, which is how male dominance was established. But over time this relationship has evolved: education, knowledge and skills have become all-important. I am resolutely feminist, and I am delighted to see more and more young women taking up senior positions. I have had the honour of meeting heads of state who are women, and I encourage you, my young friends, to take an active role in the political and economic life of your country, so that you will be in key positions to forge ahead with the Revolution of Compassion.

Accept leadership roles, for we need you to promote love and compassion. Realise my dream, that the 200 nations of the world will be governed one day by women. There will be less war, violence, and economic and social injustice. And whatever you do, you must not assume that in order to reach high office, and stay there, you need to adopt the most shameful masculine behaviours. Genuine strength is rooted in love and compassion. The more you exercise power in this way, the more violence will decrease. Young women of the millennium: I am calling on you to take your place at the vanguard of the mother of all revolutions.

ACKNOWLEDGING THE FAILURE OF ALL RELIGIONS

When I call on you to bring on the Revolution of Compassion, I am not speaking to you in the name of an ideology. I do not believe in ideologies – those systems of preconceived ideas that are applied to reality and the means by which political parties in power impose authority. Ideology is all the more dangerous because it permeates all sectors of society. Not only can you no longer discern it, your world view is unconsciously shaped by it.

Nor do I speak to you about the Revolution of Compassion as a Buddhist, as the Dalai Lama, or as a Tibetan. I am addressing you as a human being, asking you to never forget that you too are, first and foremost, a human being, before you are American, European, African, or a member of a particular religious or ethnic group. These characteristics are secondary: do not let them dominate. If I say 'I am a monk' or 'I am a Buddhist' or 'I am a Tibetan', these are subordinate realities to the fact that I am above all a human being.

To state the obvious: we are all members of one great human family. Our quarrels arise from secondary causes. You must build close relationships based on trust and understanding and mutual support, without getting waylaid by cultural, philosophical and religious differences, or by matters of faith. Being *human* is fundamental. Having been born *human* will remain a fact until the day you die. Other less important characteristics are subject to the winds of uncertainty.

In November 2015, after the Paris terrorist attacks, I faced up to the failure of religion. Every religion persists in cultivating that which divides us, instead of uniting us around what brings us together. None has succeeded in creating a better human being, or a better world. That is why now, in 2017, I have no qualms about telling you that there is an urgent need to go beyond religion. It is possible to live without religion, but can one live without love and compassion? The answer is no. As science has proved, the need for compassion is a fundamental biological human imperative.

COLLECTIVE INTELLIGENCE AND COMPASSION

You are young adults, facing different ideological and religious conflicts, and an economic system that overexploits natural resources without giving life's fragile matrix a chance to regenerate. Were we all to live in the same manner as do the most profligate on the earth,[7] more than five planets would be needed! Sixty-seven billionaires grab as much wealth as half the world's population. This is totally unrealistic; totally unacceptable.

So how are you going to deal with a senseless situation that is a consequence of pathological individualism? The only way forward is to bring on a Revolution of Compassion, which will breathe new life into democracy by extending solidarity. Place compassion at the heart of social life; develop new collaborative models that connect local communities with the global networking community. Make good use of collective intelligence, based on sharing. And above all, be the generation that acts. You may be the first generation in history to face the very real possibility of the extinction of life on our shared planet, but you are also the last one that will be able to do something about it. After you have gone, it will be too late.

To bring on a Revolution of Compassion requires awareness. You, the children of the earth's ecosystem, are living in the early years of the third millennium. The world is your home, humanity is your family. Take up the ideas behind international consciousness movements and push their rationale as far as it can go. Cultivate a sense of collective vigilance for every act of consumption, evaluating its energy footprint. Learn about the production methods of everyday things, how to recycle them, and their planetary impact.

It seems harmless enough to use disposable plastic cutlery, upgrade your mobile phone, enjoy a steak or a portion of chicken nuggets. One plastic bottle weighs just a few grams. All well and good, but those few grams are added to all the other bottles used by seven billion humans. The end result? Every second, 209 kilos of plastic are poured into the oceans, much of which ends up in the stomachs of birds and marine mammals that die in agony by the thousands along the shoreline. They die of hunger, their bellies filled with bottles, plastic cups, toothbrushes, cigarette lighters . . . all of which have passed through our hands.

YOU ARE
A PART OF
THE WORLD
AS MUCH
AS
THE WORLD
IS A PART
OF YOU

Another example: to produce a single kilogram of beef, fifteen kilograms of cereal and fifty litres of water are needed. Two-thirds of the world's arable land is cultivated to feed the cattle destined for the dinner plate in rich countries. These modes of production are criminal, and responsible for a famine that would end immediately if we all became vegetarians. A single day without meat in the United States would, for example, enable twenty-five million people to be fed for a year. So broaden your horizons and think, without losing sight of the complexity of the various interconnected factors.

This information, and more besides, is available in an instant via the social media that you are so fond of and which gives you access to an astonishing quantity of collective intelligence. Events that happen in one country affect people all over the world: this is the new reality of our time. It is essential that we be aware of our connection to seven billion other people and all the ecosystems that regulate our survival. Individualistic, egocentric attitudes are dangerous because they are not based on reality. I invite you, therefore, to pursue a process of inner transformation that acknowledges the interconnectivity of life. You are a part of the world as much as the world is a part of you. When you change as an individual, you change the world. Becoming aware of our interdependence will eventually lead to a decrease in violence, since taking an interest in others is in your interest too.

EGOTISM IS AGAINST NATURE

Being conscious entails not being in thrall to either emotion or fantasy. Violence, filmed with special effects, is doubtless bewitching. You see an average of 2,600 murders a year on your screens, whereas in real life you will not, I hope, see a single one. Witnessing the murderous violence of terrorist attacks makes you realise how hateful it is. Understand that the violence of video entertainment is a fantasy that benefits an industry that feeds off your fears. It is essential that you recognise this. I would like you to be the first generation to practise what I call *emotional hygiene*. You have been taught to be mindful of what you eat; to avoid foods and behaviours that are harmful to your health. Of course, this is important. But I have advocated that we also teach young children to understand rather than to repress their emotions. Pilot studies have started up in the United States, Canada and India. Think about it, and you will realise that you are responsible for most of the problems you face during your life. Why? Because you allow yourselves to be carried away by the repetitive patterns of destructive emotions. Being aware of this is crucial. This is why I launched the *Atlas of Emotions* in May 2016.[8] This is a comprehensive and precise mapping of emotional states, scientifically realised by my friend Dr Paul Ekman, professor of psychology and head of a team of 149 specialists. Visit the website, use the interactive map that is designed to guide you through the convolutions of your feelings, and let me know your reactions. The *Atlas* should be able to help you assess the impact of demands and outside events on your psychological state. For example, an argument will trigger aggression. As the sense of irritation grows, you must learn to recognise the signs: you get louder, becoming angry and sometimes violent. The *Atlas* should therefore teach you how to prevent, then eliminate, negative and self-destructive feelings in order to then be able to cultivate positive emotions.

My classical education in Buddhist thought taught me about the laws of interdependence, and the human potential for infinite compassion. Our prayers include the *Four Immeasurables*: love, compassion, joy and equanimity. Yet over and above

WHEN YOU
CHANGE
AS AN
INDIVIDUAL,
YOU CHANGE
THE WORLD

religion, contemporary physics has afforded me a glimpse of the infinite quality of these states of consciousness from a different angle. I learned about this particularly through my conversations with the Indian nuclear physicist Raja Ramanna. He explained to me that he discovered the uncertainty principle of quantum mechanics in the thought of the great Buddhist saint, Nagarjuna, who developed the philosophy of 'conditioned co-production' or 'interdependent origination'. Quantum vision confirms the ancestral intuition that interdependence exists at a subtle level of extreme intricacy. Even in your most subtle levels of consciousness, you resonate with the solar system, the Milky Way and the cosmos, way beyond anything you could imagine. Before your birth, during your life, and after the death of your physical body, your cells vibrate with the universe, the limits of which are unknown. Your thoughts and your feelings go far beyond what is imaginable.

Do not think that the practice of altruism amounts to self-neglect or deprivation. On the contrary, you will find that by doing good to others, you are doing good to yourself, thanks to the principle of interdependence. And so you will develop a serene, impartial temperament, and come to realise that egotism is against nature since it flies in the face of the fundamental reality of interdependence. I encourage you to become aware of how, in your own life, self-centredness closes doors, while altruism opens them.

Western philosophy, ideology, politics and economic theory have spread the belief that competition, fuelled by rivalry, envy, jealousy and resentment, imparts a creativity and dynamism to society. The twentieth century has exacerbated destructive competitiveness. People live together in a way that is underpinned by mutual indifference and withdrawal into the self. I certainly admire the tremendous growth of Western societies, but I deplore the fact that their ideology led your parents' generation to ignore the law of interdependence that is the corollary of compassion. It is particularly conspicuous in wealthy countries, where the majority of people enjoy a very high standard of living, all the while remaining terribly isolated. Is it not paradoxical that, despite having so many neighbours, many elderly people are reduced to expressing affection only to their cats and dogs? I ask you to refocus your social and human relationships towards greater consideration and loving-kindness.

4

WHAT CAN YOU DO FOR THE WORLD?

My young friends, you are probably wondering how to start a Revolution of Compassion. It is an inner process, though this does not mean that it will not impact the outside world. On the contrary, its consequences will go well beyond those of the French, Bolshevik or Chinese revolutions – and they were the most extreme of all time. The Great Day of Compassion will not happen without the impetus of your generation, and that of your children. I have spoken about the neurobiological basis of compassion, which makes you attuned to the suffering of yourself and other people, and so enables you to give comfort. The question is how to extend this human propensity beyond your loved ones, to unknown or even hostile people?

PRACTISE COMPASSION LIKE AN OLYMPIAN

This issue is addressed by the science of compassion, which was developed in the laboratories of various leading North American universities.[9] Richard Davidson, professor of psychology and psychiatry, is an eminent initiator. When he came to see me in Dharamsala for the first time in 1992, he confessed to practising meditation 'in the closet' because it was not taken seriously by his colleagues. He outlined the basis of his work on depression and psychological disorders. I pointed out that much as it was important to study the pathologies of the human mind, it would be good to research how to foster positive mental attitudes. I am convinced that one can train oneself in the art of compassion, love and happiness; indeed, I do it myself as part of my contemplative practice. Richard Davidson considered this suggestion, and reoriented his research. To begin with he didn't talk much about what he was doing, but this situation has reversed over twenty-five years. Research grants now flow through his department where a very real science of compassion is being developed.

By comparing animal and human behaviour, researchers can observe how cognitive abilities and analytical reasoning contribute towards the development of compassion. If you watch yourself, you will notice a five-level sequence in your compassionate response. Level one is cognitive: you recognise the suffering of others; level two is emotional: you are concerned about the suffering; level three is intentional: there is a desire to relieve it; level four, you focus your attention on the suffering of others; level five is behavioural, as you take concrete action to alleviate suffering. Identifying these five phases is the first part of the process of practising systematic compassion.[10]

THE DAY
IS NEAR
WHEN YOUR
GENERATION
WILL HAVE
CONSIGNED
WAR TO THE
ASH HEAP
OF HISTORY

Focus on becoming elite athletes of compassion. You will improve your performance through regular practice. Since the early 2000s, cerebral plasticity – the ability to transform the structure, chemistry and functioning of the brain through repeated and progressive exercises – has been clinically proven by neuroscientists. In other words, through practising specific exercises, you can develop a form of unconditional compassion. Here are two examples:

The first is that of a monk, Lopön-la. Detained for eighteen years in a Chinese labour camp, he lived his final years in my home, Namgyal monastery, in Dharamsala. He confided to me that he faced one danger in particular during his incarceration. I thought he was referring to the possibility of losing his life because of torture and ill treatment. But no! The danger was of losing his compassion for his torturers. For Lopön-la never stopped cultivating love for all beings, including his tormentors.

The second example is my hero, Richard Moore. As a ten-year-old child in Londonderry, in Northern Ireland, he was blinded by a rubber bullet fired by a British soldier. His uncle was killed a few days later by British paratroopers who opened fire on demonstrators at the Bloody Sunday protest march of 30 January 1972, against the policy of interning people suspected of being involved with the Irish Republican Army. Despite all this, he managed to forgive the soldier who shot him, and they met and became friends. Richard went on to found a charity that helps children and young people caught in the crossfire of global poverty, injustice and inequality.[11] This is a fine example of the immense degree of humanity to which compassion can raise you. It is an unstoppable force for forgiveness and reconciliation.

Be assured, you do not have to experience such ordeals, or be a monk, Buddhist or Tibetan, to attain this level of immeasurable,

loving, limitless compassion. You can all get there. Firstly, I say to you: 'Compassion should be the driving force of your lives!' You need to fundamentally change your understanding of human nature. If your generation develops the scientifically based conviction that every human being has a good and generous heart, imagine the profound outcome – how society would be imbued with a positive vision of humanity! When society as a whole is imbued with a positive vision of humanity, you will see contemporary power struggles transformed into a caring economy based on mutual trust and common interests.
An ethics of consideration, based on the universal human values of benevolence, tolerance, generosity, kindness, forgiveness, non-violence, will replace the current ethics of fault-finding and prohibition, which sustain the fear of punishment. And you will give your children a holistic education based on reason and loving-kindness.

A UNIVERSAL RESPONSIBILITY

Cultivated on a personal level, altruism encourages the individual to take responsibility on a global level. I was delighted when some young French YouTubers came to interview me about universal responsibility on 19 April 2017. The fifteen-and-a-half-year-old girl, Adèle Castillon, flexed her muscles theatrically and asked, 'What can I do for the world, with my teeny tiny biceps?' I answered that with such small arms she probably could not do much. I then suggested that she adjust her mindset to recognise that every action, every word and every thought has a global resonance. You experience this through messaging on the internet. Each and every one of you has global scope and expression. As a result, the exercise of individual freedom confers on you certain responsibilities and duties, along with various rights, on a global scale.

Be aware that the future of humanity does not depend exclusively on politicians, the executive officers of huge corporations, or the United Nations. The future is in the hands of all those who recognise themselves as being part of 'we, the world's seven billion people'. Individuals cannot solve the world's problems on their own. Without resorting to coercion, or playing the blame game, and always respecting pluralism, it is by the power of example that you will inspire other young people. The number of responsible individuals around you will rise from ten to a hundred to a thousand, and then many thousands. You will see an improvement in the situation of our planet. You and your children will live in this world of which I dream, but which I doubtless will not live to see.

The current problems have arisen mainly because of neglecting the wellbeing of the human family and the earth's ecosystem. Remember: universal responsibility affects

EVERY
ACTION,
EVERY
WORD
AND EVERY
THOUGHT
HAS A
GLOBAL
RESONANCE

not only human beings, but all non-human sentient beings as well. As a child, my teachers taught me to take care of the natural world. I grew up fully aware that everything that moves is sentient, and that pain, pleasure and joy are related to consciousness. No sentient being wants to suffer. In Buddhist practice we are so used to compassion – the desire to end all suffering – that we are careful not to attack or destroy any form of life, including plant life, which we treat with love and respect. But you, my young friends, have grown up in a world proud of its technological prowess, and convinced that nature must be controlled and even changed. This is a serious mistake. Such an attitude is not at all realistic and is scientific only in name. You are part of nature and compassion decrees that you take care of it as much as you do yourselves.

I am calling on you to bring on a revolution motivated by compassion, for the sake of your own children and future generations. When Westerners speak of 'humanity', they are generally referring to the present. Indeed, past generations of humankind count for little. That of the future is yet to come. All that matters from a Western perspective is today's generation and its immediate interests. But responsibility is universal only if it encompasses consideration for those who come after us. We cannot overlook the fact that the global population, which tripled in the twentieth century, will have multiplied two or threefold by the end of this century.

According to current patterns of growth, the development of the global economy entails excessively high levels of energy consumption, carbon dioxide emissions and deforestation. If we do not change our behaviour there will be environmental degradation across the globe, surpassing everything that we have seen so far. I have read scientific studies: they give us only three years to drastically reduce our current rates of consumption, which are the cause of extreme carbon dioxide emissions. By 2020 it will already be too late. Global warming is out of control; fatal heat waves will be triggered across all five continents, along with a rise in sea levels. Time is not on our side, which is why I am calling on all young millennials to hasten this radical revolution.

My young friends, brothers and sisters, in the course of my life I have been witness to our changing world. Today we face such dangers that it is vital that we do not bury our heads in the sand. For those environmental problems that have a natural cause, or that are seismic, unstoppable catastrophes, you will not necessarily manage to find solutions. And because of global warming, calamities such as hurricanes, tsunamis, floods, droughts and landslides will only increase in intensity. The only solution will be to face it all with

THIS IS THE
NEW WORLD
THAT
YOU WILL
BEQUEATH
TO YOUR
CHILDREN

courage and determination, standing shoulder to shoulder with your fellow citizens, and showing fraternal solidarity and loving-kindness towards the most vulnerable.

It is only through mutual support and cooperation that you will be able to contain disasters that are caused by economic and social injustice and are fuelled by greed, selfishness and other negative states of mind. If you shift your consciousness towards greater benevolence and responsibility, you will find real solutions. The earth is giving you clear signs of the sweeping consequences of unconscious human behaviour. For the first time in history, the future of humanity depends on the upcoming generation: yours. You are responsible for the wellbeing of billions of humans and all manner of living species sharing the adventure of life on earth. It is up to you to protect natural resources and guard over air, water, oceans, forests, fauna and flora. To do so, it is essential that you realise your potential for love and compassion in order to care for the earth. Learn to love it through sharing it, rather than striving to possess it, and thereby destroying it.

No doubt, it will take another twenty or thirty years for the Revolution of Compassion to generate the necessary changes in human behaviour. But after that change comes about, you will have the joy of witnessing the emergence of a compassionate and accountable humanity. This is the new world that you will bequeath to your children and to your children's children. They will grow up in a united human family, aware of being one body, one consciousness. Guard your youthful enthusiasm and optimism as you move towards a fairer and happier tomorrow.

5

THE WORLD OF COMPASSION EXISTS

EPILOGUE BY SOFIA STRIL-REVER

19 April 2017, morning. Four young French YouTubers[12] have just had an extraordinary experience. I have brought them to meet the spiritual guide of the Tibetan people to discuss this book. Although they do not know much about the Dalai Lama, they are fascinated by him, and they know that he embodies a benevolent humanity. They had been inspired to meet him after they read the Charter of Universal Responsibility,[13] which moved them to seek new ways of thinking, and gave them the keys to unlock the door so they could help create a better world. The Dalai Lama suggested that, since they are French, why don't they start the revolution our world needs in France? Although he was

addressing the young YouTubers, he turned towards me as he spoke. Afterwards he reached out to embrace me, calling me 'my long-time friend!'

This reference to the French Revolution took me back to a few months earlier: 13 September 2016. In collaboration with the Paris Bar Association, I organised a meeting with the Dalai Lama and 350 lawyers and international environmental experts, to be held during the Global Forum on Environment.[14] During my introductory speech, I mentioned the 1789 Revolution and the fact that lawyers spearheaded it. The next day, in the Senate, with a knowing smile in my direction, the Dalai Lama spoke of himself as a secular disciple of the French Revolution. So I interpreted his concluding words to the YouTubers as being an invitation to help focus his call to the youth of today for a revolution. He confirmed as much and a new meeting was arranged three months later.

THE DALAI LAMA'S REVOLUTION

July 2017. Ladakh, northern India. The Dalai Lama received me at Shewatsel Phodrang, 'supreme palace of peace'. During our encounter he looked at me with great concentration, transferring a very particular intense energy to me – namely the energy of the Revolution of Compassion that so motivates him.

The Dalai Lama has himself undergone the Revolution of Compassion, and he has now entrusted me with its message. In preparation for our encounter, I had gathered together those mind-training aphorisms that make up the Tibetan Buddhist spiritual practice known as *Lojong*. This word encompasses a set of mental exercises which progressively refocuses consciousness so that it ceases to function in a self-centred manner and becomes spontaneously altruistic. Even so, the Dalai Lama insisted that for the young generation of the twenty-first century, training in compassion must be based on neuroscientific research that is validated by collective experience and common sense. First, because science is universalist in spirit, whereas religion is divisive. Second, because young people today have a scientific mindset. Third, because in order to change their way of thinking, they must know how the mind works, and have the tools of neuroscience at their disposal to rally all their knowledge and understanding.

The Dalai Lama could have drawn on Buddhist psychology – which is underpinned by 2,500 years of introspective phenomenology. Defining himself as part-Buddhist monk and part-scientist, over the last thirty years he has endeavoured to show how the collaboration between neuroscience and the Buddhist science of the mind gives a renewed understanding of the mind, medicine and instruction through the introduction of meditation to research laboratories, hospitals

COMPASSION
EXISTS.
IT IS HIDING
WITHIN THE
WORLD
AROUND US.

and schools. But when speaking to the millennial generation, he put himself in their place. What would be the best way to guide them through the current crisis? The answer came: by going beyond religion, and basing the learning of compassion on human reason and common sense, without reference to any belief system. As I listened to him, only too aware of the subversive nature of his message and the urgent need to pass it on, I measured how far we had come since we first worked together on his book, back in 2009: *My Spiritual Autobiography*. I thought about this in detail during the weeks that followed, as I replayed the highlights of our discussion in my mind so that I could internalise them and write this book.

TO EXIST IS TO COEXIST

The ethos of the Revolution of Compassion resonated strongly in me because my thinking has been nourished by discussions with lawyers and law-makers, initially during the 2015 United Nations Climate Change Conference when I presented the Dalai Lama's message about ecology.[15] That collaboration resulted in a series of seminars entitled 'Law and Consciousness', emphasising the link between a *collective* commitment based on law, and making a conscious *individual* commitment. The coming together of these two elements – a vital necessity, given the current environmental crisis – lies in the recognition of our multiple interdependencies with the earth's ecosystem and the need to take universal responsibility for it.

One evening, after an encounter with the Dalai Lama, I experienced this in a very personal way, as I walked barefoot along the sandy riverbed of the Indus in Ladakh. The great Himalayan mountain range was on the horizon. Solid and massive, its giant flanks were whipped by the fury of the winds, while its peaks pierced the arc of the sky. But the vision of the mineral landscape faded at my contact with the flowing water, brimming with life at my feet.

I became one with the living water of the 'Lion River'[16] that springs from a snow-and-ice matrix near Mount Kailash, a sacred mountain scattered with votive shrines built by devout pilgrims.

I became one with the tremendous flow of this fifty-million-year-old body of water and its vertiginous gorges that stretch for over 3,000 kilometres from the Land of Snows, through Ladakh and Baltistan, along the Karakorum and the Hindu Kush, before veering south to irrigate the plains of Punjab and Sindh, and then finally embracing the Arabian Sea with all seven arms of its vast delta.

I became one with the water lapping at my ankles. I felt the pain of the Tibetans who live on the 'Roof of the World', an open-air prison where religious and secular children, teenagers, women and men of all ages regularly practise self-immolation as an act of resistance in defiance of the dictatorship of the People's Republic of China. To date, over 150 human torches have burned in the face of the indifference of the world's nations.

I became one with the powerful voice of the river as it swept along its irrepressible song of compassion, calling on humanity to find the loving, shining source of its original loving-kindness.

In these Himalayan landscapes, I discovered that existing means coexisting according to the unitary system of life. A few months earlier, on 21 March 2017, the state of Uttarakhand in northern India had granted the status of 'living entity' to the Ganges, its tributary the Yamuna, and all the rivers in its territory. The High Court gave rivers, streams, torrents and waterfalls the same status and legal rights as people, thus making them our brothers and sisters at the heart of the earth's ecosystem. The Indian judges placed them under the protection of 'parents with a human face', responsible for guaranteeing their health and wellbeing.[17]

I felt this kinship with the Indus with an intimacy that was all the more poignant because the river is seriously under threat. Downstream, the industrial pollution and overpopulation on the outskirts of cities have transformed it into a giant open sewer. The aquatic fauna has all but vanished as dams ravage the ecosystems that form a single entity within the Indus. Only a thousand dolphins now survive in its waters. Its delta has been devastated by deforestation and rising sea levels as a result of global warming. Agricultural land and creeks of submerged mangroves have led to the forced migration of more than a million refugees. Along the entire length of the river, a dividing line is being drawn between the nourishing vitality of nature and the plundering by humankind that is causing a devastating ecocide.[18]

On my return flight from Ladakh, I was overjoyed to read in Air India's *Shubh Yatra* in-flight magazine the words of Uma Bharti, Minister for Water Resources, River Development and Ganga Rejuvenation in the Union Government of India: 'I believe that the issue of water should be approached with love not aggression. We are already cooperating with Nepal and Bangladesh, and it is in this spirit that we will work with our other neighbours.' This declaration is part of a major revolution, based on the concept that nature itself has rights, which is now being ratified by legal practitioners. Governments are following suit. On 19 September 2017, French president Emmanuel Macron launched the Global Environment Pact[19] at the UN General Assembly, a critical next step following on from the Paris Agreement.

Forty years ago, the anthropologist Claude Lévi-Strauss observed presciently that the rights of man would need to be limited at the

LEARN TO
LOVE THE
EARTH
THROUGH
SHARING IT,
RATHER THAN
STRIVING TO
POSSESS IT

point when privileging them would lead to the demise of animal or vegetable species.[20] Today we need a new social contract that takes into account the current state of the law, which is only focused on the present and on humankind. This new social contract needs to anticipate future global devastation in a world where one person in every seven is predicted to be a climate change refugee by 2050.[21]

THE REVOLUTION OF COMPASSION HAS DAWNED

'We *know* about environmental problems. But are we *mindful* of them?' wonders the lawyer Patricia Savin, presciently.[22] This is where the Revolution of Compassion takes on its full significance. The legal transition needs to be accompanied by an inner transition that changes our whole way of thinking, placing altruism at the heart of our lives. The reforms that are being developed may be very pertinent in themselves, but they are not enough. It is imperative that we move on from a culture of performance, competition and rivalry towards a culture of sharing and solidarity. This calls for a revolution: the Revolution of Compassion. It has already begun. It has other names, other spokespersons.

Matthieu Ricard calls it the Altruistic Revolution. He theorises it in his book *Altruism: The Power of Compassion to Change Yourself and the World,*[23] supported by over a thousand scientific references demonstrating that compassion modifies the structures, chemistry and functions of the brain. He translates these insights into action through his humanitarian work in Asia[24] and his commitment to the cause of animal rights.[25]

According to the philosopher Abdennour Bidar, the Revolution of Compassion is the Fraternity Revolution; he calls on us to 'repair together the damaged fabric of the world'.[26] Noting the crisis in interpersonal relationships, 'the mother of all crises', in 'a world that

THE
REVOLUTION
OF
COMPASSION
IS A MILLION
QUIET
REVOLUTIONS

is multidamaged and polyfractured', he describes it as the need to 'transform friendship into a political project'.

The Revolution of Compassion is also an intrinsic part of the Earth Democracy movement, according to Indian physicist and ecologist Vandana Shiva.[27] She sets out ten principles of human sovereignty over seeds, water, food, land and forests, so that humanity can practise a genuine and profound form of democracy in tune with all of life.

The Revolution of Compassion is also known as 'a million quiet revolutions',[28] breathing hope into the concept of an engagement with civil society and, more specifically, with young people, in favour of more environmentally aware, participative and compassionate societies.

The Revolution of Compassion has dawned. It is not a dream. A compassionate world exists. It is hiding within the world around us.[29]

In the course of my conversations with the Dalai Lama in Ladakh in July 2017, I promised him that I would do everything I could to ensure his appeal would be heard by as many people as possible. I recalled the pride of the four young YouTubers to whom I had introduced him three months earlier, their attention and emotion when in the presence of the Dalai Lama, who addressed both their hearts and their minds. These young people discovered another world, far from their frenetic Western lives. Even time was different. This book is my contribution to their world in the process of being born.

Dharamsala, 2 October 2017

THE CHARTER OF UNIVERSAL RESPONSIBILITY[30]

EXTRACTS

The Revolution of Compassion involves three moments of realisation and eleven commitments for life, as set out in the Charter of Universal Responsibility.

First moment of realisation:

INNER PEACE AND THE SHARED REALITY OF LIFE

I was born on this earth, a child of life, at the heart of the cosmos.

My genetic codes incorporate messages from the universe. I am linked to all living things in the shared reality of life. Their wellbeing depends on the balance of the ecosystems, which are themselves dependent on the peace that reigns in the heart of men and women, and the spirit of justice in human society, where no one shall be cast aside, or afflicted by hunger, poverty or deprivation. In a spirit of equality, free from prejudice, material attachment and hatred, I commit to playing my part in maintaining and re-establishing the harmony of life.

May peace and inner healing be present in every single one of my actions, dedicated to the good of all existence, both human and non-human. This is an appeal to all living beings to participate in the joy of universal love that is the lifeblood of life.

Second moment of realisation:

OUR INNER HUMANITY

I was born on this earth, a child of life, at the heart of humanity, my family.

I am motivated to act for the good of all living beings purely by altruism, and by accepting my universal responsibility. Inner peace, love and compassion are not only ways of expressing a noble ideal, but also of offering pragmatic solutions to issues we face in this new reality, as a means of guaranteeing our collective interests in the face of the loosening of social bonds and the breakdown of social solidarity.

Recognising the necessity of cooperation enables me to understand that the most secure basis for worldwide sustainable development is based on both the individual and the shared practice of inner peace, love and compassion. I revitalise hope and confidence in the shared destiny of humanity.

Third moment of realisation:

SATYAGRAHA, THE FORCE OF TRUTH

I was born on this earth, a child of life, at the heart of the great peace of the natural world.

In this era of the internet and globalisation, I am aware of how I am being manipulated and instrumentalised by techno-economic culture; and of my obligation to embody the wisdom of universal responsibility, based on the power of truth and love, what Mahatma Gandhi called Satyagraha. Satyagraha is my weapon in the non-violent combat against injustice. The moment that truth passes through me to express itself, I become invincible. By living Satyagraha on a daily basis, I become, amongst others and with the help of others, an architect of peace, justice and truth. As a citizen of the world, I assume this new civic bond of universal responsibility. In this way, future generations will one day be witness to this new world to which I aspire, but which I may never see. According to my means, I will try my hardest, in a spirit of peace and love, to construct a new reality, that of a compassionate earth.

END NOTES

1. According to the Tibetan system, at birth a person is one year old
2. Professor George Gerbner's (1919–2005) theory showing how violence on screen contributes to violence in the real world, as well as feelings of anxiety and insecurity
3. For example, the African Union, ASEAN (Asia), ALENA, MERCOSUR, AEA, CARICOM. Complete list: www.wikipedia.org/wiki/Liste_d%27organisations_internationales
4. Mind & Life XXIII conference, September 2011. The debates that took place during the conference emphasised the intersection between Buddhism and science in order to enhance our understanding of the nature of reality, www.mindandlife.org
5. The Juliana vs. US climate lawsuit filed in September 2015 at Oregon District Court, with the support of climate scientist James Hansen, www.ourchildrentrust.org
6. See a discussion of this point in Daniel Goleman, *A Force for Good: The Dalai Lama's Vision for Our World*, 'Women as Leaders', Bloomsbury Publishing, 2015

7. According to figures supplied by the Global Footprint Network in 2017
8. www.atlastofemotions.org
9. Notably at the Center for Compassion and Altruism Research and Education at Stanford University, http://ccare.stanford.edu; the Emory-Tibet Science Initiative, https://tibet.emory.edu; and at MIT's The Dalai Lama Center for Ethics and Transformative Values, http://thecenter.mit.edu
10. Cognitive-Based Compassion Training (CBCT) was initiated in 1998 by the Dalai Lama at the Center for Multidisciplinary and Contemplative Studies at Emory University, in partnership with Geshe Lobsang Negi, PhD, senior lecturer in Emory University's Department of Religion, and the Drepung Loseling Monastery in South India
11. https://www.childrenincrossfire.org/
12. Adèle Castillon, Seb la Frite, Valentin Reverdi and Sofyan Boudouni, accompanied by the film director Anaïs Deban. See the video *Séjour en Inde* by Seb la Frite, www.youtube.com/watch?v=wmT0h3e6Am0
13. Published in the book *The New Reality: The Age of Universal Responsibility*, Les Arènes, 2016
14. The Universal Responsibility, Law and Environment conference was attended by special guest Robert Badinter, along with Frédéric Sicard, president of the Paris Bar, Dominique Attias, vice-president of the Paris Bar, lawyers Patricia Savin, Corinne Lepage, Yann Aguila, Yvon Martinet, and founding president of

Peace and Universal Responsibility Europe (PURE) Khoa Nguyen, www.universal-responsibility.org

15. The United Nations Framework Convention on Climate Change (COP 21) held in December 2015
16. 'Senghe Tsangpo' in Tibetan
17. Valérie Cabanes, *Homo Natura*, Buchet-Chastel, 2017
18. For a definition of ecocide, cf. website www .endecocide.org
19. The Global Environment Pact was drafted by approximately 100 international experts under the guidance of French lawyer Yann Aguila, a former judge and member of the Council of State, president of the Environment 21 Commission of the Club des Juristes and secretary general of the Committee of Experts for the Pact, www.pactenvironment.org
20. Claude Lévi-Strauss, *Le Monde*, 21 January 1979
21. *The Charter for Environmental Refugees* by the lawyer Yvon Martinet (www.lawandconsciousness.org) and the *Universal Declaration of the Rights of Humanity* by the lawyer Corinne Lepage (www.droitshumanite.fr)
22. President of Orée and director of the Sustainable Development Commission of the Paris Bar, speaking at the Climate and Conscience conference, 31 August 2017, www.lawandconsciousness.org
23. Matthieu Ricard, *Altruism: The Power of Compassion to Change Yourself and the World*, Atlantic Books, 2015; Matthieu Ricard and Wolf Singer, *Beyond the Self: Conversations between Buddhism and Neurosciences*, The MIT Press, 2017

24. Through the charity Karuna-Shechen, www.karuna-shechen.org
25. Matthieu Ricard, *A Plea for the Animals*, Shambhala, 2017
26. Author of *Plaidoyer Pour la Fraternité*, Albin Michel, 2015; *Les Tisserands*, Les Liens Qui Libèrent, 2016; *Quelles Valeurs Partager et Transmettre Aujourd'hui?*, Albin Michel, 2016. Founder of the movement Fraternité Générale, www.fraternite-generale.fr
27. Rewarded for her commitment in 1993 by the Right Livelihood Award, the alternative Nobel Prize, www.navdanya.org
28. Bénédicte Manier, *Un Million de Révolutions Tranquilles*, Les Liens Qui Libèrent, 2016
29. Echoing the words of the poet Paul Éluard: 'Another world exists. It is hidden within this one.'
30. At the request of the Dalai Lama and in the spirit of his teachings, the Charter of Universal Responsibility has been written by Sofia Stril-Rever, in collaboration with the venerable Samdhong Rinpoche, Professor Robert Thurman of Columbia University, New York, and Professor Eric Itzkin, Deputy Director of Immovable Heritage, Johannesburg. The text was finalized with the Dalai Lama in Oxford, in September 2015. Full text, Nouvelle réalité, Les Arènes, 2016.

ABOUT THE AUTHORS

The Dalai Lama is the spiritual leader of Tibet. From 1959, Tenzin Gyatso, the Fourteenth Dalai Lama, has lived in exile in Dharamsala, in the north of India, since the invasion of Tibet by China. He was awarded the Nobel Peace Prize in 1989. www.dalailama.com

Sofia Stril-Rever has coauthored four books with the Dalai Lama (including his *My Spiritual Autobiography*, translated into some twenty languages). Together with the Paris Bar Association, she has initiated the 'Law and Consciousness' study group to address environmental challenges according to the idea of universal responsibility, a concept promoted by the Dalai Lama as the key to human survival in the twenty-first century. http://www.lawandconsciousness.org

Share your thoughts on the book

on Twitter

on Instagram

by tagging @DalaiLama and using the hashtag

#CallForRevolution